"I AM"
ADORATIONS
AND
AFFIRMATIONS

"I AM" ACTIVITY
OF
SAINT GERMAIN FOUNDATION

The "I AM" Religious Activity represents the Original, Permanent, and Highest Source of the Ascended Masters' Instruction on the Great Laws of Life, as first offered to the western world by the Ascended Master Saint Germain, through His Accredited Messengers, Mr. and Mrs. Guy W. Ballard.

In the early 1930s the Ballards established Saint Germain Foundation and Saint Germain Press, Inc. which under Saint Germain's Guidance, have expanded into worldwide organizations that offer to mankind the true Ascended Master Teachings on the Great Cosmic Word, "I AM"! Saint Germain Foundation strives to keep the "I AM" Ascended Master Instruction in Its pure, unadulterated form, free from any human interpretation, personal monetary gain, or proselytizing, as It is a Gift from the Great Ascended Masters and Cosmic Beings to bring Illumination and Perfection to mankind.

Hundreds of "I AM" Temples and Sanctuaries exist throughout the world, where the Teachings are applied in "I AM" Decree Groups. The Books of the Saint Germain Series are available in many libraries, bookstores, or directly from Saint Germain Press (address below). For further information, please contact:

SAINT GERMAIN FOUNDATION
SAINT GERMAIN PRESS
1120 Stonehedge Drive
Schaumburg, Illinois 60194
United States of America
(847) 882-7400 or (800) 662-2800
www.SaintGermainFoundation.org
www.SaintGermainPress.com

SAINT GERMAIN SERIES
VOLUME 5
Part I

"I AM"
ADORATIONS
AND
AFFIRMATIONS

BY
CHANERA

SAINT GERMAIN PRESS

© 1937 Saint Germain Foundation
2015 Printing
Printed in the United States of America

Library of Congress Cataloging-in-Publication Data

Chanera, 1886-1971.
    ["I AM" adorations and affirmations]
    "I AM" adorations and affirmations ; "I AM" decrees / by Chanera.
    - - 3rd ed.
        p. cm. - - (The Saint Germain series ; v. 5)
    1. I AM Religious Activity   I. Chanera, 1886-1971.   "I AM"
decrees.   II. Title: "I AM" adorations and affirmations.
III. Title: "I AM" decrees   IV. Series.
    BP605.I18 C47   1991
    299' .93 - - dc20   91-20332   CIP
ISBN-13: 978-1-878891-25-9 (softbound-pocket)
ISBN-13: 978-1-878891-24-2 (casebound)
ISBN-13: 978-1-878891-27-3 (e-book)

CONTENTS

PART I

✧ ✧ ✧

DEDICATION

This series of Books is dedicated in Eternal Love and Gratitude to our Beloved Ascended Masters, Saint Germain, Jesus, Nada, the Great Divine Director, and also to the Great White Brotherhood, the Brotherhood at the Royal Teton, the Brotherhood of Mount Shasta, the Great Ones from Venus, and those other Ascended Masters whose loving help has been direct and without limit.

$$\Diamond \, \Diamond \, \Diamond$$

FOREWORD

At the request of many Students, this Book of "*'I AM' Adorations and Affirmations*" is given to the public. They are sent out with the Decree that: "All who read or use these Commands shall be held, by the Love of the 'Mighty I AM Presence,' in constant conscious communion with that Master Presence of Light within themselves."

Every time the Great Creative Word, "I AM"! is read, thought or spoken, the feeling released should be that of an exclamation because "I AM"! is the Life from the Great Central Sun announcing Its Presence through the individual who thinks, speaks or feels that Great Eternal Fiat of Life's existence. Therefore, always release that strong powerful feeling whenever you use the Great Creative Word, "I AM."

In this way, the limitless Energy of Life releases through you to fulfill your Call for assistance and Perfection.

If the Student will read these Decrees slowly and with deep, deep feeling in each word as you come to it, you will have Instantaneous Manifestations when you can feel the meaning in each Word deeply enough.

The word "human," throughout this Series of Books, is always used to mean discordant. When the word "annihilate" is used, it always means the annihilation of discord or imperfection, for no one can annihilate God, Good, Who is Life; and the annihilation of discord can only bring Happiness and Perfection as a result to all.

This Book is charged with and carries to Its readers the Rays of Light and Love from the Ascended Masters, Saint Germain, Jesus, Nada, the Great Divine Director, and the other Ascended Masters who are pouring Their Radiance through this Activity, to which Godfré Ray King, Lotus Ray King and Donald Ray King add their Triple Activity of Light and Love from the "Mighty I AM Presence" for the Illumination, Freedom, Mastery and Perfection of all who read or contact It, for America and the world.

Chanera

The first duty of the outer self is to turn to the "Beloved Mighty I AM Presence" and ask for orders.

"I AM"
ADORATIONS
AND
AFFIRMATIONS

PART I

"I AM"
ACKNOWLEDGMENT

The "Mighty I AM Presence" is within this Book! Let all of Earth keep silent before It and be at Peace, in humble, grateful, loving, adoring Obedience unto that blazing Light, our Supreme Source.

Keep us, O "Mighty I AM Presence," humble before Thee, positive to the world, and forever in the Service of the Ascended Host of Light.

All "I AM," or have, or ever hope to be or have is Thine, O "Mighty I AM Presence"! Come forth, in the Fullness of Thy Power! Control and hold Dominion in this body, brain, mind and will! Pour forth Thy Full Glory on Earth, as Thou art in Heaven! Do Thou so illumine me by Thy Light that there is none of me but all of Thee.

3

There is a "Presence" in man, and the Light from that Presence is his Understanding. That "Presence," that Light, and that Understanding is "I AM"; and "I AM" That "I AM"!

I call unto Thee, O "Mighty I AM Presence," Thou Great Central Sun, Thou Heart of Infinity! Pour forth Thy Mighty Flame of Divine Love throughout humanity and the Earth! Set the feet of mankind once again securely upon the Pathway of Light, and anchor their attention forever upon Thee, the Great Love Star in the Heart of each one! Lift their Hearts unto the Heights whence cometh all Help, and bring them back into the Happiness, Freedom and Perfection which is their birthright.

The "Mighty I AM Presence" is within this Holy Temple; let all of Earth keep silent before that Blazing Glory, and be at peace! in humble, grateful, loving, adoring obedience unto that Supreme Source.

O Presence of the Diamond Heart! come forth in the Fullness of Thy Power! Release Thy Victory everywhere, and seal all within Thy Heart, forever.

CLASS ACKNOWLEDGMENT

This Class *(Group)* is a "Temple of Light"!
The "Heart of Divine Love"!
The "Secret Breath of God"!
The "Altar of Eternal Peace"!
The "Focus of the Great Silence"!
The "Ocean of Limitless Power"!
The "Treasure Chest of the Almighty"!
The "Sun of Everlasting Freedom"!
The "Throne Room of Infinite Life"!
The "Gift of the 'Mighty I AM Presence,' "
        forever!

*Note: The above can be used for healing
the body, as well as for the Class Work.*

In the Fullness of the "Presence"
Is the Love that you require,
In the Fullness of the "Presence"
Are the things that you desire!

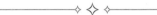

✧ ✧ ✧

BROTHERS OF THE GOLDEN ROBE

Great Beings of the Golden Robe,
  Transcendent Ones of Love!
Enfold all those upon the Earth
  Who call to Thee above.

Guard well the children seeking Light,
  Release through them Thy Power;
To those who know and need Thee, COME!
  Be with them every hour.

Reveal the Glory of Thy Height,
  The Victory Thou hast won,
Blaze forth Thy Full Dominion NOW,
  Great Masters from the Sun.

Show all Thy Mantles of Love's Light
  So golden hued and pure;
Enfold us, as we call to Thee,
  And make our Victory sure!

Great Beings of the Golden Robe,
  In Love's Own Sacred Name,
Awaken everyone on Earth
  To LIGHT, the "Great I AM"!

✧ ◇ ✧

THE DIAMOND HEART

O Presence of the Diamond Heart!
  In Victory now I come,
Bearing the "Cup of Liquid Light,"
  All Earth's battles won.
I raise my sword and now step through;
  Within the Flame, I bow to You,
And You, the Heart of Light in all,
  Reveal to me the Great, the small.
Upon my shoulders, blazing bright
  You place my Cape of dazzling Light;
And I, at last, all blest and Free,
  Know only Love, myself, as Thee.

O Presence of the Diamond Heart,
  All Ecstasy Supreme;
Thy Joy now all encompassing,
  My own Life's Radiant Stream,
Is ever pouring out Its Light—
  All—All Perfection too;
"I AM"! Thy Presence, Lord of Life,
  O Great Love Flame, just You!
In Love, in Peace, in Glorious Power,
  In all realms and all space,
I hold Thy Hand, Thou Source of All,
  "I AM"! Thy own Bright Face.

◇ ◇ ◇

LORDS OF THE BLUE FLAME

Lords of the Flame, the Sacred Fire,
 The Great, Great Ray of Blue!
Flood forth o'er our America,
 Earth's atmosphere step through.

From Thy Great Heart of Love so pure,
 Of Wisdom and ALL Power,
Blaze forth Thy Dazzling Cosmic Light,
 Protect Her every hour!

Through Angel Host of Beings bright
 Send forth the Great Blue Flame
To fill our loved America
 With Victory, through "I AM"!

That Mighty Glorious Sacred Name,
 For all Eternity,
Shall evermore now fill the Earth,
 Till all mankind is Free!

"I AM"! says Life to all that is;
"I AM"! Love's Gift to all;
"I AM"! the Mighty Flame of Blue,
"I AM"! Its Cosmic Call!

✧ ✦ ✧

THE LOVE STAR

THE LOVE STAR–*"The Secret"*

Love Star, Love Star, Love Star bright,
Love Star, Love Star, blaze through us Thy Might;
Love Star, Love Star, our own Hearts' Light!
Love Star, Love Star, enfold us tonight.

THE LOVE STAR–*"The Call"*

O Love Star! we call Thee,
　　Thou Jewel from the Sun,
O Heart of Creation,
　　Thou Glorious One!
Come now in Thy Splendor,
　　Flash forth Thy Great Flame,
Burst all bonds asunder,
　　Speak forth the Great Name!
Declare now Thy Victory
　　And set this Earth Free;
Reveal Thy Dominion,
　　Thyself let all see.

From Thy Blazing Altar,
    Light's Greeting first came,
The Voice of God's Presence,
    Almighty, "I AM"!

THE LOVE STAR–*"The Presence"*

The Love Star–His Presence!
    All silent, serene,
In Glory transcendent
    While blessing the scene;
Stands radiant with Power
    Its Rays pulsing bright,
Chaste ribbons of silver
    Adorning the night;
Caressing, encircling,
    Enfolding the sod;
Light! tying the Earth to the
    Feet of her God!
The Master Christ Presence,
    Incarnate in man;
The Source of all Freedom,
    The Blest Word, "I AM"!

THE LOVE STAR–*"The ALL"*

The Love Star, the Flame-breath,
   The Great Heart in all,
Comes forth in Its Splendor
   To answer each call;
Reveals now Its Vict'ry,
   In all Realms Its Light,
Clothes us in Its Glory
   And Radiance bright;
Let all then surrender
   Their might and their power,
Through loving obedience
   Be raised *now* this hour–
Forevermore Master!
   Eternally free,
The Blest "I AM Presence,"
   The Great Cosmic Key.

◇ ✧ ◇

ADORATIONS

THE LOVE STAR–*"The Secret"*

Love Star, Love Star, Love Star bright,
Love Star, Love Star, blaze through us Thy Might;
Love Star, Love Star, our own Hearts' Light!
Love Star, Love Star, enfold us tonight.

THE GRAIL

We, as One, offer ourselves as a Grail, a
Crystal Cup of Thy Mighty Presence, O "Beloved
I AM"! Keep It filled full to overflowing with Thy
Glorious Life! Pour out through us Thy Mighty
Love and Light, letting It flow forth as an ocean of
Thy Blazing Essence, raising all into Thy Limitless
Perfection forever.

ENFOLDED

I wear pure golden sandals
    With ribbons of Light,
A crown made of Sun Rays,
    A cloak of God's Might.
I carry a Scepter,
    My Focus of Power;
I pour forth the Pure Christ
    Each moment, each hour.

Note: We offer the following poem in Love and Adoration to our Beloved Ascended Master Saint Germain, for whom we call forth the Infinite Eternal Light and Love from the "Mighty I AM Presence," to bless Him with Its Mightiest Eternal Victory for the wonderful Gift of Himself to the Children of Light, that they, too, may manifest the same Perfection and Freedom which He is.

THE ASCENDED MASTER, SAINT GERMAIN

O Blest Saint Germain, Dear,
    Thou Holy Great One,
We love Thee and bless Thee,
    Thou God from the Sun.

We feel Thee and see Thee,
    The Work Thou hast done,
For the Cup Thou dost carry
    O'erflows from the "ONE."

We praise Thee and greet Thee,
    Thou Great Lord of Light,
And raise now the Scepter
    To Thy glorious Height.

We wield all Love's Power,
    Love's Wisdom and Might;
Blaze through us forever
    Thy Flame, Dazzling Bright.

Let all my Love flow back to Thee,
Thou Holy, Great God Flame of me!
Expand Thy Light and set me Free,
Let me Thyself forever *Be!*

Thou Adorable Supreme "I AM"! expand, expand, and again expand Thy Light in Eternal Glory through me.

"Beloved I AM Presence"! I offer my service to Thee in the capacity for which I am best fitted.

O "Mighty I AM Presence"! I love Thee, I bless Thee for the joy of Thy Glorious Light that lifts me beyond my outer self.

**You have the Opulence of the
Universe to draw from!**

◇ ◇ ◇

INVOCATIONS

THE LOVE STAR–*"The Call"*

O Love Star! we call Thee,
   Thou Jewel from the Sun,
O Heart of Creation,
   Thou Glorious One!
Come now in Thy Splendor,
   Flash forth Thy Great Flame,
Burst all bonds asunder,
   Speak forth the Great Name!
Declare now Thy Victory
   And set this Earth Free;
Reveal Thy Dominion,
   Thyself let all see.
From Thy Blazing Altar
   Light's Greeting first came,
The Voice of God's Presence,
   Almighty, "I AM"!

✧
✧
✧

Open, O Thou World-sustaining Sun, the entrance unto Truth! Hidden by the bars of Dazzling Light, soften the Radiation of Thy Illuminating Splendor, that we may behold Thy True Being. From the unreal lead us on to the Real, and unveil the human creation of the physical world, that we may know the Victory of the Ascension.

✧

My "Mighty I AM Presence"! Let me hear Thee and see Thee and feel Thee, and let me hold Thy Hand. Come! walk with me and talk with me. Oh, let me understand, know and remember all Reality. Let me forget all unreality and know myself as Thee and Thyself in me, as all of God's Great Blazing Light, for all Eternity.

RAISE US!

Raise us! Raise us! Raise us!
O Great "I AM" to Thee.
Raise us! Raise us! Raise us!
And set us ever Free.
Raise us! Raise us! Raise us!
To Thy Great Heights Divine.
Raise us! Raise us! Raise us!
We are forever Thine.

"Mighty I AM Presence"! project into this condition Thy Mighty Ascended Master Miracle-working Lightning of Divine Love. Blast everything human, its cause and effect into annihilation forever, and see that only Thy Miracles of Eternal Peace, Love, Harmony, Illumination, Protection and Perfection ever come out of it to all concerned.

"Mighty I AM Presence"! come forth this instant and charge this entire condition (*person, place or thing*) with the Fullness of Thyself! Project into it Thy Miracle-working Lightning of Divine Love and compel only Ascended Master Miracles of Perfection to come out of it to everyone; and keep them eternally sustained and ever expanding.

"Mighty I AM Presence"! come through me! Do this thing perfectly! and see that I expand Thy Perfection, forever.

"Mighty I AM Presence"! take me into your Heart tonight while my body sleeps! Instruct me in the fullness of the Ascended Masters' Understanding of the "I AM Presence"! See that I bring back that Instruction clearly into all my outer activity when I awaken in the morning, and make me always express Thy Full Perfection forever.

"Mighty I AM Presence"! come forth in the Full Dominion of the combined Ascended Host, and make every educational activity a crystal clear channel through which the Ascended Masters can always work for the Purity, Protection and Perfection of the Youth of America and the world.

"Mighty I AM Presence"! come forth and project Thy Lightning of Divine Love in Its most powerful, dynamic Activity into every educational channel on earth! Annihilate forever all teaching that is not the fullness of the Ascended Masters' Truth and Consciousness! Fill the minds and hearts of all mankind with the "Light of God That Never Fails," compelling Perfection to come forth everywhere to bless all forever with the "Power of a Thousand Suns."

"Mighty I AM Presence"! descend into this place! Do Thy Perfect Work and hold Thy Full Dominion here forever.

✧

"Mighty I AM Presence"! sweep into this _____! Annihilate everything human within it! Release Thy Mighty Power! Compel a Mighty Miracle of Perfection to come out of it to all concerned, and keep it forever sustained by Thy Mighty Presence which "I AM."

"Mighty I AM Presence"! charge me and my world with the Violet Consuming Flame of Divine Love which consumes all that is undesirable; and keep me clothed forever with Thy Almighty Perfection.

"Mighty I AM Presence"! take out of me all doubt and fear, and charge me with Thy Eternal Love, Courage, Strength, Protection, and ever-expanding Perfection.

"Mighty I AM Presence"! sweep in here, make all things new instantly and hold Thy Full Dominion forever!

"Mighty I AM Presence"! raise everything in my being and world into the Heart of Thy Secret Love Star and see that I abide in Thy Great Peace and Self-control forever.

"Mighty I AM Presence"! lock me within Thy Perfect Self-control and hold me there forever.

✧

The "Mighty I AM Presence" is always the only Governing Intelligence here.

"Mighty I AM Presence"! turn me from that human experience! Take it into oblivion and make me forget it forever!

"Mighty I AM Presence"! seize possession and control of my attention! Keep it upon Thee and Thy Perfection forever, and do not let it ever wander again.

"Mighty I AM Presence"! see that I never miss or disobey a Direction from Thee! See that I do only that which expands Thy Perfection everywhere forever.

"Mighty I AM Presence"! make and keep me infinitely sensitive to Thee and Thy Perfection, forever in the Heart of Thy Love, and absolutely non-recordant to everything else.

"Mighty I AM Presence"! take this doubt out of me! Make me see, feel and BE the fullness of this Truth and Thy Perfection forever!

"Mighty I AM Presence"! protect forever every Student in this Group, and all under this Radiation, and hold each one steady in his effort to reach Perfection.

"Mighty I AM Presence"! take me to the Golden Temple of Light tonight while my body sleeps! Charge my being and world with Its Light, Energy and Perfection, and see that I bring back Its Full Perfection into my physical body and outer activity when I awaken.

"Mighty I AM Presence"! put me into my Perfect Work now, and make me do it perfectly.

"Mighty I AM Presence"! show me what You want me to do now, and make me do it perfectly.

"Mighty I AM Presence"! consume in me and my world all doubt, fear, jealousy, pride, resentment, irritation, criticism, condemnation and judgment, their cause and effect, replacing them by the Fullness of the Perfection which Thou art, keeping It Self-sustained in the ever expanding Light of Thy Glorious Presence.

"Mighty I AM Presence"! shatter and consume forever this discordant condition in and with _____! Annihilate its cause and effect throughout the Earth forever, and see that it never touches our lives or world again.

"Mighty I AM Presence"! seize possession of that (or this) mind and body! Enter in! Hold Your Dominion; and compel the attention to be anchored forever upon Thee and Thy Eternal Perfection.

"Mighty I AM Presence"! seize possession of these eyes! Look through them perfectly! Make them see and visualize only Perfection, forever Self-sustained.

"Mighty I AM Presence"! take possession of and command me forever; see that nothing ever gets my attention again but Thee and Thy Perfection.

"Mighty I AM Presence"! take possession of my mind, body, being and world forever! Lock them against the recognition of all human creation! Fasten my attention entirely upon Thee and Thy Perfection! Cut me free forever from the magnetic pull of Earth, the things of Earth and all human creation. Fill me with Thyself, Thy Full Ascended Master Consciousness and Mastery and hold Thy Full Eternal Dominion.

"Mighty I AM Presence"! take complete control of my Being, world, and activity! and see that I make my Ascension in this embodiment; for "I AM" the Resurrection and the Life! "I AM" the Ascension in the Light!

Use once an hour:

"Mighty I AM Presence"! come forth, charge my being and world with the Light and Love from the Secret Love Star, and keep It eternally sustained.

"Mighty I AM Presence"! I here, now, and forever give You all Power! I give You all Obedience! Take charge of this mind and body! Prepare it to become the Ascended Master and see that I make my Ascension now.

"Mighty I AM Presence"! charge me with the Ascended Masters' Feeling and Victory of the Ascension.

"Mighty I AM Presence"! see that I make my Ascension now!

"Mighty I AM Presence"! take me into Your Heart and reveal to me and through me the Fullness of Thyself, instantly, infinitely, and eternally manifest.

"Mighty I AM Intelligence"! bring this Eternal Victory of Light and Love to pass now, in all Thy Blazing Glory.

"Mighty I AM Presence"! lock my mind and feeling forever against everything but Thy full "Presence" and Its Perfect Activity, instantly and eternally manifest.

"Mighty I AM Presence"! descend into this Thy mind and body. Take full Conscious Control this instant of all its activities; and hold Thy Dominion and Victory here forever!

"Mighty I AM Presence"! draw me within the most Blazing Light of Your Heart, and seal me there forever, that only Your Fullest Perfection may express.

"Mighty I AM Presence"! come forth! Charge my being and world with that Light and Love as of a thousand suns, and crowd my path with showers and showers of Blessings and Ascended Master Miracles and Victories of Light, forever.

Come forth, "Mighty I AM Presence"! Manifest Thy Mighty Miracles of Perfection instantly; and see that only the greatest, most transcendent good comes out of this occurrence forever.

For mistakes in others:

"Mighty I AM Presence"! forgive them for they know not what they do; and do Thou, my own God Flame, see that I do not do it too.

"Mighty I AM Presence"! forgive my mistakes! Come forth in Thy Infinite Power, and transmute that energy into a Mighty Ascended Master Miracle of Perfection made manifest today.

"Mighty I AM Presence"! henceforth, You are the Doer! Come forth and take command here forever!

"Mighty I AM Presence"! take complete possession of my attention and my feelings, and fill them entirely with Thyself.

"Mighty I AM Presence"! come forth and manifest Thy Supreme Authority of Divine Love in my being and world forever.

"Mighty I AM Presence"! show me Your Perfect Channel for this activity. Open it to me through Divine Love, and put me to work within it at once, producing Your Perfection forever.

Make me a new Heart, O "Mighty I AM Presence,"
and let me feel the Fullness of Thyself within me.

"Mighty I AM Presence"! charge me full to
  overflowing forever with:
    Inexhaustible Strength and Energy,
    Indestructible Health,
    Invincible Protection,
    Irresistible Divine Love,
    Inescapable Prosperity,
    Ascended Master Consciousness,
    Illumination,
    Freedom, and
    Use of Thy Full Power instantly and
      eternally manifest.

For business dealings:

"Mighty I AM Presence"! I want the Perfection
of Your World brought into mine! Take command
here and produce Your Victory forever!

"Mighty I AM Presence"! You are the only Presence, Power, and Intelligence acting in my business. Protect and take it forward to Your Complete Success and Perfection, forever self-sustained in Blazing, Glorious Light, manifesting Mighty Miracles of Perfection, now.

"Mighty I AM Presence"! charge my entire mind and body with Thy Ascended Master Consciousness and keep It eternally sustained.

"Mighty I AM Presence"! see that the flesh of this body never again records any human quality; and keep it forever filled only with Thyself, and express Thy Glorious Perfection.

"Mighty I AM Presence"! these are Your hands. Pour forth through them always Thy Healing Miracles and Full Perfection.

"Mighty I AM Presence"! this is Your brain; these are Your hands; play with Your Mighty Perfection and produce Your Mighty Glory and Music of the Spheres!

"Mighty I AM Presence"! illumine this for me and tell me Your Full Truth concerning it.

"Mighty I AM Presence"! make me fully comprehend this which I wish to know and understand right now.

Come forth, Thou "Mighty I AM Presence"! and blaze through me now and forever "The Light of God That Never Fails."

"Mighty I AM Presence"! take me deep within the Heart of the Great Central Sun! Charge my consciousness with that Light! Teach me the Full Ascended Masters' Knowledge of the Flame; and see that I awaken with that Knowledge in my brain consciousness.

"Mighty I AM Presence"! I call unto Thee as never before! Answer Thou me with the Full Freedom of Thyself.

"Mighty I AM Presence"! put me in my own right harmonious place and sustain me there.

"Mighty I AM Presence"! I thank Thee for all the money that comes into my hands and use or that touches my world! I accept it as Thy Messenger of Love and Balance! Charge it with Thy Purity, Love and Blessing without limit; and see that it brings only Thy Freedom and Perfection everywhere in the world.

"Mighty I AM Presence"! move everywhere before me today, and do all for me and through me perfectly!

"Mighty I AM Presence"! protect me from the human suggestions of the outer world, that I may go forth only accepting Thy Mighty Self and Thy Perfection forever.

"Mighty I AM Presence"! surround America forever by Thy Circle of the Ascended Masters' Consuming Flame of Divine Love, which never admits anything unlike Thee or Thy Perfection.

"Mighty I AM Presence" and Mighty Ascended Masters! come forth in all outer activity! Seize control of America, the government, her people, and her resources! Hold them forever in the Heart of Thy Perfection; and bless all with Thy Happiness and Transcendent Light.

"Mighty I AM Presence"! come into this condition and solve it perfectly.

✧

Do not use your energy to condemn politicians, but say many times a day for America:

In the Name of the "Mighty I AM Presence," I call the Light and Love of the Ascended Masters into the White House, into the National Capital, into every State in the Union, into the Hearts and minds of all politicians to produce Perfection NOW; and bring everything into Light's Victory of Divine Love.

In the Name of the "Mighty I AM Presence," I charge the minds and feelings of everybody in America with Saint Germain's Ascended Master Consciousness and Perfection. God bless, illumine, perfect and set them Free in the Service of the Light forever!

"Mighty I AM Presence"! shatter and consume all activity of the sinister force in America, its cause and effect, replacing it forever by the Eternal Perfection of the Ascended Masters' "Light of God That Never Fails."

Mighty Ascended Masters and Great Legions of Light! fill America with that Light, Love, Protection and Power as of a thousand suns, and keep Her forever Invincible to all but Thy Mighty Perfection.

✧

"Mighty I AM Presence"! You are the Power! You are the Intelligence acting here! Come forth and manage this outer activity now and forever with Ascended Master Management.

"Mighty I AM Presence"! come forth and annihilate this discordant action, its cause and effect, and put Thy Divine Perfection in its place forever.

"Mighty I AM Presence"! seize that energy! Requalify it by Your Divine Love and Perfection; and anchor it in my world, maintaining Ascended Master Protection and Perfection for me forever.

"Mighty I AM Presence"! either silence these discordant people, or put them where they belong; and bless them by Thy Power of Divine Love!

"Mighty I AM Presence"! come forth and manage this thing! Seize my attention and my feelings and hold them upon Thee forever!

"Mighty I AM Presence"! qualify every thought and feeling about this with the Ascended Masters' Accomplishment, Victory and Perfection.

My "Mighty I AM Presence"! Thou art my way, my protection, my defense and my deliverance from all disturbing conditions, and the instantaneous annihilation of their cause! Thou, my God-Victorious "Presence," come forth and manifest with Full Power through this mind and body forever.

Raise your hands to the "Mighty I AM Presence" and say:

"Mighty I AM Presence," come forth here! Silence that human nonsense, mentally and physically, forever.

"Mighty I AM Presence"! come into my mind and body this day! Manage me and hold Thy Supreme Dominion, forever.

"Mighty I AM Presence"! come forth! Right this condition and seal it in Thy Heart forever!

"Mighty I AM Presence"! produce Your Divine Love here and sustain It forever.

I call my "Mighty I AM Presence" and Saint Germain's Ascended Master Consciousness to come forth and solve this _____ for me forever!

"Mighty I AM Presence"! come forth! Govern and solve this situation harmoniously forever.

"Mighty I AM Presence"! shut the door of my being and world forever against all human creation, and instantly annihilate all that attempts to open it.

"Mighty I AM Presence"! take care of my human creation, and see that I make the Ascension now, as quickly as possible.

"Mighty I AM Presence"! release Your Love and Light as of a Thousand Suns and maintain Your Perfection here forever!

"Mighty I AM Presence"! come forth! Charge my being and world every second of this day and forever with Ascended Master Perfection, instantly and eternally manifest.

"Mighty I AM Presence"! sweep my intellect clear from everything but Thee and Thy Perfection, and keep it so forever.

"Mighty I AM Presence"! charge my mind and body with Your Mighty Perfection forever.

"Mighty I AM Presence"! lock my mind and feelings forever against everything but Thy Full Perfection and Its Eternal Activity.

_____(name)_____: I, the "Mighty I AM Presence," speak to Thee: Awaken Thou! into the Perfection of Life!

"Mighty I AM Presence"! project Your Divine Love through me today, and forever pour out Your Full Dominion.

"Mighty I AM Presence"! command Divine Love to take full command of all my activity, and bring everything into Divine Order through Divine Love!

"Mighty I AM Presence"! charge me so full of Divine Love that every person, place, condition and thing I contact becomes instantly harmonious and obedient to Thee and Thy Perfection; and hold Thy Full Dominion forever.

Make me a new Heart, O "Mighty I AM Presence"! and keep the feeling of Thy Presence, Thy Light, Love and Victory within me forever.

"Mighty I AM Presence"! show me the Full Ascended Master Knowledge of everything concerning the Seven Mighty Elohim.

"Mighty I AM Presence"! make me Thy Supreme In-breathing and Outpouring of the Love from the Great Central Sun, forever.

"Mighty I AM Presence"! charge me with all the Perfection there is, everywhere present, visible and invisible; and keep It eternally sustained.

"Mighty I AM Presence"! take me to the Great Central Sun, and charge my brain, body and world with such tremendous Divine Love, Wisdom and Power that It sweeps everything else before It; and make me express Thy Full Dominion.

"Mighty I AM Presence"! make me always Your most dynamic Action of Divine Love in Full Ascended Master Dominion through this brain and body, forever Self-sustained.

"Mighty I AM Presence"! raise the Liquid Light in my body. Take It back into Thyself, and produce Perfection in me forever!

"Mighty I AM Presence"! charge my body with Thy Light, until my face becomes Radiant and Self-luminous.

"Mighty I AM Presence"! seize possession of these eyes. Look through them perfectly, and see that they visualize only Perfection, forever Self-sustained!

"Mighty I AM Presence"! I call unto Thee! Answer Thou me! Blaze through my being and world forever Thy Full Dominion! Bring everything into Divine Order through Divine Love instantly, and keep it forever Self-sustained. Take complete control of my being and world! Manage my every activity with Ascended Master Management and compel all to manifest Thy Perfection, forever Self-sustained.

"Mighty I AM Presence"! charge me so full of Divine Love that every person, place, condition and thing I contact becomes instantly Harmonious and Obedient to the "I AM Presence."

"Mighty I AM Presence"! qualify all with Thy Perfection; and charge this Work with Saint Germain's Complete Ascended Master Consciousness, Protection and Perfection forever. I call unto Thee to come forth in the Fullness of Thy Power, and produce limitless Miracles and Victories of Thy Light forever.

"Mighty I AM Presence"! take charge of my attention! Anchor it into the Heart of Your Light and keep it there eternally.

"Mighty I AM Presence"! show me Your Way. It seems to be my duty to do this thing; so show me Your Way.

"Mighty I AM Presence"! come forth! Illumine this thing for me and show me the Ascended Master Way.

"Mighty I AM Presence"! lock me in Thy Eternal, Perfect, Self-control that always consumes all human qualities and habits. This instant and forevermore manage all my activities and work, with Ascended Master Perfection. Release into my hands and outer use all Thy stored-up Treasures! Keep all forever Self-sustained through Thy Divine Love and express the Fullness of Thy Victory.

"Mighty I AM Presence"! take me within Thyself, instruct me, and cause me to retain the Full Memory of these Inner Instructions.

"Mighty I AM Presence"! come forth! Lock my being and world forever against all human creation! Keep my attention anchored upon the Ascended Master Consciousness and Perfection of the "I AM," the "Light of God That Never Fails."

"Mighty I AM Presence"! God in me, is my certain Victory, and I cannot fail!

"Mighty I AM Presence"! clothe me in the Ascended Masters' Consciousness of Divine Love forever!

"Mighty I AM Presence"! take me into Your Ascended Master Body and teach me the use of the Light Rays, that Thy Perfection may set me Free and reign forever upon Earth.

"Mighty I AM Presence"! charge my aura with instantaneous Healing to everybody that comes into my presence, and set all free in the Service of the Light.

"Mighty I AM Presence"! Stand guard and prevent any disembodied individual from coming into my aura at any time! Let nothing touch my consciousness but the Ascended Masters and the Angelic Host!

"Mighty, Majestic, Supreme I AM Presence"! in Thy great calm, serene Dominion I rest, yielding not to any human thing.

"Mighty I AM Presence"! charge me always with Your Mightiest, Dynamic Action of Divine Love, in Full Ascended Master Dominion through this brain and body, forever Self-sustained.

"Mighty I AM Presence"! come forth and charge this house *(home or activity)* with the combined Love, Peace and Protection of the Ascended Host, and hold It there forever.

"Mighty I AM Presence"! see that this home, this environment, and all connected with it are governed harmoniously, and that all who enter manifest only the Ascended Master Activity.

"Mighty I AM Presence"! I wash my hands of all things human forever!

"Mighty I AM Presence"! insulate my mind, body, being and world forever from all human creation.

At least three times a day, stand on the floor with hands upraised and say:

"Mighty I AM Presence"! fill me with Your Love, Power and Perfect Intelligent Direction.

If confused, simply say:

"Mighty I AM Presence"! Light! Light! Light! Let there be more Light, the "Light of God That Never Fails"!

All activity in schools and colleges:

"Mighty I AM Presence"! blaze Thy Violet Lightning of Divine Love through all educational channels! Annihilate all wrong teaching of every kind, and its cause and effect throughout the Earth! Take possession of the brains and bodies of all students! Produce Thy Purity, Thy Perfection, Thy Protection! Illumine all by the Light of Thy Truth and keep It forever Self-sustained in the Eternal Glory and Victory of Thy Love.

"Mighty I AM Presence"! give me the time to do this thing *(loving Thee)*, and make me do it in that time.

"Mighty I AM Presence"! give me this Perfect _____ *(thing or condition)* through Divine Love.

Visualize America as a Great Heart of Golden Flame, the outer Radiance violet surrounded by a Wall of Steely White Light. Make the Call:

Mighty Divine Director and Legions of Light! Fill America with that Light, Love, Protection, and Power as of a Thousand Suns that never fail, and keep Her forever Invincible to all but Thy Mighty Perfection.

"Mighty I AM Presence"! awaken all mankind! open all channels! and see that everyone accepts the Fullness of Thy Mighty "Presence" now, and receives Thy Eternal Freedom.

"Mighty I AM Presence"! make me feel Thy Rays of Divine Love every minute.

"Mighty I AM Presence"! I thank You for Your Life, Your Energy, and all You are constantly giving to me!

"Mighty I AM Presence"! raise and use all my Life Energy in Thy Limitless Intelligent Action forever.

"Mighty I AM Presence"! come into my mind and body this day and manage me forever!

If you want Freedom, you must *give* it—FIRST.

AFFIRMATIONS

THE LOVE STAR–*"The Presence"*

The Love Star, His "Presence"!
    All silent, serene,
In Glory transcendent
    While blessing the scene;
Stands radiant with Power
    Its Rays pulsing bright;
Chaste ribbons of silver
    Adorning the night.
Caressing, encircling,
    Enfolding the sod;
Light! tying the Earth to the
    Feet of her God.
The Master Christ Presence
    Incarnate in man,
The Source of all Freedom,
    The Blest Word, "I AM"!

INVOCATION TO THE FLAME

"I AM"! the Eternal Flame of Life, a White-Fire Being from the Heart of God! In-breathing the Great Love Breath of the Almighty, I dwell within my Golden Ray from the Great Central Sun! Crowned with the Diamond Rays of Attainment, I abide upon my Sacred Lotus Throne of Light, letting my Love flow out unto all creation! "I AM" a Sun in the Palace of Infinite Light! My world, the Altar of Infinite Space! My Radiance, the Peace of the Great Solar Quiet! "I AM" the Undying Flame of Life everywhere, the Great Eternal Joy and Glory and Perfection of existence. "I AM"! "I AM"! "I AM"! Three times three "I AM"!

"I AM"! Elohim, Elohim, Elohim,

Elohim, Elohim, Elohim, Elohim!

Seven times seven "I AM," E-LO-HIM!

Note: Students affirm:

"I AM"! the Ascended Masters' Eternal Acceptance of this.

"I AM"! always the Majestic Presence and Miracle-working Power of Divine Love that transcends every human concept; blazing through me and to me forever all the Perfection from within Its Heart, with the Power of a Thousand Suns.

"I AM"! the Eternal Ceaseless Flow of the Blazing Light from my "I AM Presence" through my mind and body.

"I AM"! forever God-commanded.

Make your outer mind continually acknowledge:

"I AM"! through the veil now!

"I AM"! the Ascended Master Presence I desire to be, and "I AM"! the Ascended Master Consciousness of this Victory.

(Then be sure the personality does not think, say, feel, see, hear, or do anything unlike the Perfection of the Ascended Masters.)

"I AM" the "Presence" raising the atomic structure of this body to the Ascended Masters' full Illumination and Liberation.

"I AM"! the Mighty Flame of Life, raising all in my being and world into the Diamond Heart, and holding it there forever.

"I AM"! the Ascended Master Consciousness everywhere that does all things perfectly today.

"I AM"! the Ascended Master Control of all my energy forever.

"I AM"! Christ! God in Action! The "Light of God That Never Fails," in the Fullness of Its Eternal Victory and Dominion.

"I AM" the "Presence" qualifying all my feeling with the Full Perfection and Expansion of the Ascended Master Consciousness.

"I AM"! the Ascended Master Control of that habit in you, _____.

"I AM"! the Pure Electronic Body of Light, illumining every person, place, condition and thing wherever I am or pass by, and all my thought rests upon.

"I AM"! the positive, rich, full, clear, perfect, loving Voice of the Ascended Masters, and I speak only as They speak, now and forever.

"I AM"! all the vigor and resilience of Eternal Youth and Beauty, and all the Wisdom, Strength, Courage, Power and Self-control of my "I AM Presence," expressing only Full Ascended Master Perfection forever.

To help others:

Here pal: "I AM"! the Strength in you that conquers that.

Here pal: "I AM"! a mountain of Light, Love and Strength in you that never fails.

"I AM"! always the Limitless Peace of the Eternal.

"The Light of God Never Fails" and "I AM"! that Light—God in Action—for God in me is always my certain Eternal Victory.

"I AM"! the instant, the hour and the day of Fulfillment.

"I AM" the "Presence" qualifying this with a Mountain of Light that casts no shadow, and in which are all good things.

Whenever you think of what you want, say:

"I AM" the "Presence" qualifying every thought and feeling about this with the Ascended Masters' Accomplishment and Victory.

I do know the Ascended Master Thing to do in this situation, and "I AM" the "Presence" doing it now, instantly and eternally victorious.

To human creation say:

No! Now you get out! The "Mighty I AM Presence" is in control here and I know it!

Know:

The "Mighty I AM Presence" is in and all about this person, place, condition or thing, and only God in action acts back to me.

Say to all disturbing persons, conditions or human creation:

"I AM" the "Presence" commanding Silence! Peace! and Obedience! to the "Mighty I AM Presence" forever.

"Mighty, Majestic, Supreme I AM Presence"! in Thy Great, Calm, Serene Dominion I rest forever, yielding not to any human thing.

"I AM" the "Presence" that never doubts, fears, questions, nor is uncertain concerning the instantaneous Fulfillment of my every Call to the "Mighty I AM Presence."

"I AM"! the Ascended Masters' Eternal Divine Memory.

"I AM"! the Guard, Self-sustained forever, that gives out only Truth and Perfection.

"I AM" the "Presence" of Divine Love and Intelligence, acting in all these Classes, and the Ascended Masters' Victory of Light eternally sustained.

I awake! I arise! I shine! for my Light is come! And the Glory of the "Mighty I AM Presence" is blazing and Invincible within me!

"I AM"! the Ascended Master Management of everything in my world forever.

"I AM"! always the Ascended Masters' Revelation, Acceptance and Use of all the Powers of the Being which "I AM."

"I AM"! always the unyielding, joyous Determination of the "Great I AM" releasing Perfection everywhere.

"I AM" the "Presence" of the Great Silence!

"I AM" the "Presence," Love, and Power in you that conquers that.

"I AM"! now the Full Confidence of the "Mighty I AM Presence" forever.

"I AM"! the feeling of the Great "I AM."

"I AM" the "Presence" that forgives and forgets all human mistakes forever and replaces them with the Infinite "I AM" Perfection, eternally sustained, in Blazing Glory and ever-expanding.

I do know the Ascended Master thing to do every second, every day, and I do it always.

There is no personality in my world today! There is only God in Action, the "Mighty I AM Presence."

"I AM" sealed forever in the Peace, Protection, Security, Love, Wisdom, Power, Supply and Freedom of the "Light of God That Never Fails."

"I AM"! the Almightiness of the Great Silence.

"I AM"! the Ascended Master Consciousness and ever-present Victory of all I desire to do forever.

Before going to sleep:

Through the Presence, Power and Intelligence which "I AM," I go forth while my body sleeps, feeling and experiencing the Fullness of myself as the Infinite "I AM Presence," and when my body awakens, charging it full to overflowing with the feeling of that "Presence."

"I AM"! the Freedom of the Great "I AM. "

"I AM"! eternally God-controlled every moment, every day, in everything, and every way.

Because "I AM" Thee and Thou art me, "I AM" Protected, Illumined, Supplied and Free!

What is that to me? I follow Thee, Thou Infinite "Almighty I AM Presence" forever!

Peace! Peace! Peace! Be still! "I AM"! Perfect Obedience to my Inner Will.

My eyes are the Eyes of the "Mighty I AM Presence." I see all things and through all things perfectly, and I see Perfection everywhere.

My ears are the Ears of the "Mighty I AM Presence." I listen only to the Voice of my "I AM Presence," accept only Its Truth, and hear only the Music of the Spheres perfectly forever.

The Light of the "I AM" is Mighty and does prevail, and I feel Its Victorious, Majestic Presence controlling at all times within me.

"I AM"! the Pure, Crystal Clear Mind of God the "Mighty I AM Presence" in that *(or this)*

brain and body, maintaining Ascended Master
Consciousness and Dominion there forever!

"I AM"! the Pure Sight of God, the "Mighty I AM
Presence," and I see Perfection everywhere.

"I AM" the "Presence" that does not take on
suggestions from anybody or anything about me,
but God! Good!

"I AM" the "Presence" that can and does clear
all human concepts of mankind permanently
everywhere I go, because "I AM"! God in Action.

"I AM" the "Presence" refusing all human
interference forever with this Work and Light of
the "I AM Presence" in ourselves, the Students,
or anything under this Radiation, in America and
the world.

"I AM"! always the Miracle-working Presence
in everything I desire to have done.

"I AM"! always Perfect Poise that controls
everything instantly and harmoniously through
Divine Love.

"I AM" the "Presence" that is always proof against any and every sudden disturbance forever.

"I AM" the "Presence" who is never disturbed or off guard.

Acknowledge often:

"I AM" the "Presence," commanding a Gigantic Ascended Miracle of Perfection to come out of every situation through Divine Love.

"I AM"! the Pure Mind of God, the "Mighty I AM Presence" forever!

"I AM"! the Pure Love of God, the "Mighty I AM Presence"!

"I AM"! the Pure Feeling of God, the "Mighty I AM Presence"!

"I AM"! the Pure Speech of God, the "Mighty I AM Presence"!

"I AM"! the Pure Sight of God, the "Mighty I AM Presence"!

"I AM"! the Pure Hearing of God, the "Mighty I AM Presence"! Forever, forever, and forever.

✧

"I AM"! the Resurrection, the Life, the Health, and the Light of my body, made manifest in and through my flesh today!

"I AM"! LIGHT, LIGHT, LIGHT! ALL LIGHT! This is the Master Record upon which humanity was modeled in the beginning, the Image and Likeness of God, the "Mighty I AM Presence."

"I AM"! the positive, poised, peaceful, loving control of this whole situation forever.

"I AM" the Conquering "Presence." I command this "Presence" to take control of all my affairs and produce Perfection always.

"I AM" the Controlling, Harmonizing "Presence" everywhere I move and of everything to which my thought is directed, bringing all into Divine Order through Divine Love.

"I AM"! come within the Stillness of Thy Heart! my "Mighty Majestic I AM Presence"! Keep me sealed in It forever, that only Thy Full Perfection shall always express.

"I AM"! the Ascended Master Control and Qualification of all the energy of my being and world, forever manifest in Full Power with the speed of thought.

I go forth this day with the tread of a Mighty Conqueror, Lord of Life and Victor over death and hell, Glorious, Supreme in the Great God Flame of Life, and "I AM"! Free! Forever Free!

✧

"I AM"! the Ascended Master Payment of this (of every) bill or obligation, instantly and eternally manifest through Divine Love.

"I AM"! the inescapable, inexhaustible Riches of God flowing into my hands and use today, manifest with Full Power, as a glad-free gift of Divine Love.

I refuse everything but the Fullness of God's Supply to me, NOW!

"I AM"! the Ascended Masters' Fulfillment of the Divine Law, the Law of Love, concerning this money in the handling of these _____.

✧

The Love that "I AM" greets the Love in you, and the God Flame of "I AM" comes instantly through and releases Its Perfection, forever.

"I AM"! the Fire Breath of Divine Love from the Great Secret Love Star.

"I AM" the "Presence" charging my being and world forever with the Pure Power and Feeling of the Flame of Divine Love from the Lords of the Flame from Venus, and keeping It forever manifest in Supreme Victory.

"I AM" the Majesty of Divine Love and the Ascended Master Victory in my being and world, forever Self-sustained.

"I AM" here and "I AM" there! "I AM"! Divine Love and Blessing everywhere.

---- ◇ ◇ ◇ ----

O Masters of the Diamond Heart!
I call now unto Thee!
Pour out Thy Flame forevermore,
Thy Great Love Power through me.

---- ◇ ◇ ◇ ----

"I AM" the Heartbeat of Divine Love! the Great Secret Love Breath of the "Mighty I AM Presence."

"I AM" always the Majestic Power of Pure Love that transcends every human concept, and opens the Door to me to the Light within Its Heart.

"I AM"! the Great Love Flame of the Almighty, manifest with Full Power through this, my mind and body forever.

I invoke the Full "I AM" Power and Activity of Divine Love in my being and world today and forever, manifest with the speed of thought.

Silence! Peace! and Obedience! to the "Mighty I AM Presence" forever!

"I AM" the "Presence" thinking through this mind and body forever.

"I AM" the "Presence" that nothing ever opposes.

"I AM" the "Presence" to whom there is no interference and no delay.

"I AM" the ever-present Ascended Master Protection in my being and world, that no human creation can ever break through.

"I AM"! the Ascended Masters' annihilation of this, and its cause and effect forever.

"I AM"! always the Master Presence and Eternal Victory of the "Light of God That Never Fails."

"I AM"! always surrounded by that Circle of Consuming Fire, which does not admit anything unlike the Christ, the Ascended Masters' Perfection.

Through the "Presence" which "I AM"—this thing shall cease now and forever, and is replaced by Saint Germain's Perfection.

I do accept the Full Dominion of my "Mighty I AM Presence" in my being and world forever.

Remember again and again, that as you grow into the Full Acceptance of your "Mighty I AM Presence," your outer problems will disappear; for "I AM" the "Presence" dissolving all problems permanently. Then, visualize the Mantle of Invisibility enfolding you.

"I AM" the "Mighty Presence" on guard forever.

"I AM"! the Invincible Guard; established, sustained and maintained over my mind, my body, my home, my world and my affairs forever.

"I AM"! the Ascended Master Annihilation of all human creation in my mind, body and world, now and forever.

In the Name of the "Mighty I AM," which "I AM"! I silence, shatter, and consume this human creation and its cause forever.

When necessary to discuss some discordant condition, say:

"I AM" the "Presence" withdrawing all energy

from the words and feelings expressed, and I requalify it with Thy Purity and Love and hold it in my world, maintaining Ascended Master Protection and Perfection for me.

"I AM" the "Presence" refusing acceptance of this discordant outer thing. I shut my door and it stays out.

The "Mighty I AM Presence" is my Way, my Protection, my Defense and my Deliverance from every disturbing condition, and the Release of the Full Dominion of the Ascended Masters' Light, Love and Victory in all my activities now and forever.

"I AM"! the ever-present Ascended Master Protection, that no human creation can ever break through.

The Love that "I AM" greets the Love in you, and this Pure Liquid Light comes instantly through, and heals you forever.

"I AM"! the Ascended Master Release of this Perfect Activity, Precipitation, instantly manifest with Full Power and Ascended Master Protection.

"I AM"! the All-Knowing Mind of God! I do know the right solution of this problem, and I solve it now through Divine Love.

"I AM" the "Presence" and Power in my world this day that conquers every problem by the "Light and Love of God that never fail," and that hold Its Eternal Victory and Freedom.

I place all my problems within the Heart of the "Great I AM," and "I AM" at Peace in the "Light of God That Never Fails."

"I AM"! the Mighty Ascended Master Solution of this problem, now and forever.

"I AM"! the Ascended Masters' Instantaneous Solution and Miraculous Victory in this problem, and the feeling of God control fills me forever.

"I AM" the "Presence" and Power in you that conquers this problem, for "I AM" your Supreme Victory over this human nonsense.

"I AM"! the Supreme Victory over all human consciousness forever.

I now cast all this human creation, its cause and effect into the Sea of Consuming Fire and Eternal Forgetfulness, replacing it by the Presence and Eternal Perfection of the "Great I AM."

God, the "Mighty I AM Presence," is alive within me. I do not allow that "Glorious Being" to be silenced by the doubts and fears of my human self.

"I AM"! the Ascended Masters' Attainment of Divine Love forever.

"I AM"! a Mountain of Divine Love that brings all Miracles to pass instantly at my command forever.

"I AM"! the Love and the Strength in you that conquers, and the "I AM" is your Victory!

"I AM"! always the Love of the "Great I AM" forever.

"I AM"! the Ascended Masters' Freedom of Divine Love in Full Control at all times.

"I AM" the "Presence" and limitless Focus of such Divine Love in this _____ as has never been experienced before on Earth, and "I AM" the "Presence" keeping It forever Self-sustained in Full Power.

"I AM"! the All-controlling Presence of Divine Love at all times. "I AM" the Herculean Love of the "Mighty I AM Presence," controlling and acting in Full Ascended Master Consciousness through this mind and body forever.

The Love that "I AM" greets the Love in you, and this Miracle of "I AM" comes instantly through, and blesses you with Perfection forever, for in the Fullness of that Love is the Victory you desire.

Peace! Peace! Peace be still! "I AM" this Miracle of Love's Great Will.

"I AM" this Mighty Ascended Master Miracle performed today with the speed of thought, and made manifest with Full Power. I thank Thee, "Great I AM."

"I AM" the Presence of Divine Love blessing every atom into Peace and Perfection.

"I AM"! the Presence of Divine Love perfecting everything there.

"I AM"! the Supreme In-breathing and Outpouring of the Great Love Breath of the "Mighty I AM Presence" forever.

"I AM" the "Presence" entering into, revealing and charging all my outer activity with the Music of the Spheres, Instantaneous Healing, Ascended Master Precipitation, and the Eternal Dominion of Divine Love.

"I AM"! the Ascended Masters' Instantaneous Precipitation and visible Presence of everything I desire; and no human consciousness can interfere with It.

"I AM"! the combined Presence and Power of the Ascended Host, standing like a Wall of Light, instantly annihilating everything that attempts disturbance or interference with anybody or anything under this Radiation.

Students are to feel this for each other:

"I AM" the "Presence" that loves you into your perfect Ascended Master Activity. "I AM" the "Presence" that loves you into your conscious ability to do this.

"I AM"! the Ascended Master Consciousness of Boundless Divine Love flooding all everywhere.

"I AM"! the Great Love Flame of the Almighty, manifest with Full Power through this, my mind and body forever.

"I AM" sealed within the Love Flame from the Secret Heart of God. "I AM" the "Presence" sealing you in the Love Flame from the Secret Heart of God.

"I AM"! the Overflowing Presence of Divine Love ruling everywhere.

"I AM"! the Presence and Power of the Ascended Masters' Love here which never fails.

"I AM"! the Strength, Courage, and Power to move forward steadily through all experiences whatever they may be, and remain joyous and uplifted, feeling only the Peace and Harmony at all times of the Glorious Presence which "I AM"!

"I AM"! always enfolded in the Mantle of the Master Christ; therefore, I maintain my thoughts, feelings and words free from all criticism and judgment.

Illumination of body, mind and atmosphere:

"I AM" the "Presence" illumining this mind, body and room with the Blazing Light of the Ascended Master, and keeping It forever sustained in Full Power through Divine Love.

"I AM"! Jesus Christ's Ascended Master Consciousness of my attainment of the Ascension.

Use this often, for it stills the outer activity, so you become centered in the activity of Divine Love:

"I AM"! the Commanding Presence.

"I AM" Ascended! "I AM" Ascended! "I AM" Ascended! "I AM" Ascended! in the Mighty Strength of my dauntless "Mighty I AM Presence" which is forever unconquerable, unquenchable, unalterable in Its everlasting Perfection, Mastery, Victory, and Majesty expressed through this mind and body now, which is no longer human but Divine. All earthly activity shall bow before me, be silent, and obey the Christ in me forever in the Service of the Light.

The most permanent, Perfect Way to illumine the physical body is to take the consciousness that:

"I AM" expressing and radiating the brilliant LIGHT OF GOD, the "I AM Presence," in me, and illumining this body for me.

Say to the body:

"I AM" the "Presence" commanding you to be strong and take on the Beauty of Form and Expression of the "Mighty I AM Presence" forever.

For heart trouble say:

My breath is the great Love Breath from out the Great Central Sun. My Heart is God's Heart, the very center of Divine Love, and Its Light fills me now!

"I AM" the "Light of God That Never Fails" now made permanently manifest in my flesh as Self-luminosity.

"I AM" the cleansing process always active in my mind and body, consuming all imperfection and revealing the Purity "I AM."

"I AM" the Resurrection and Life of my business, my understanding and whatever I wish to center my attention upon.

"I AM" the Resurrection, the Life and the Health of my body made manifest in my flesh today.

Hands and feet:

These are God's Hands and Feet and I charge them with the Power, Perfection and Perfect Love of the "Mighty I AM Presence" forever.

"I AM"! the Mighty Electronic Energy flowing through, filling and renewing every cell of my mind and body, right now.

"I AM" the "Presence" breathing Perfection in and through this physical flesh body forever.

The "I AM Presence" governs this physical body completely and compels it into obedience.

"I AM" the "Presence" qualifying this mind and body with absolute Perfection, and refusing acceptance to anything else.

Whatever there is of imperfection in me must get out! I qualify everything in my being and world this day with Perfection, because "I AM" Perfection!

Contemplation:

"I AM" come within the stillness of Thy Heart, my "Mighty Majestic I AM Presence"! Keep me sealed in It forever, that only Thy full Perfection shall always express.

Whatever is under the whole heaven is mine to love and to bless forever, with the Perfection of the "Mighty I AM Presence."

"I AM" the "Presence" commanding the visible and tangible Presence of the Ascended Host with us now, in the physical octave.
(Go on! Accept this, and stick to it!)

"I AM"! the Master within, governing and controlling all my thought processes in Full Christ Perfection, as I wish them to be.

"I AM" the "Presence" arranging my time in Perfect Divine Order.

"I AM" the "Presence" producing the perfect business I desire.

"I AM"! the Mighty Cosmic Light, Divine Justice and Protection acting in the minds and Hearts of individuals everywhere.

"I AM" always loving Obedience to the Light.

"I AM"! "I AM"! I know "I AM"! Free from this thing forever, no matter what it is.

"I AM"! the Ascended Master Consciousness Self-sustained that does not permit me to give out anything but that which is Perfect.

"I AM" no longer the "Babe of Christ," but the "Master Presence" grown to full stature, and I speak and command with authority.

"I AM"! the Law of Forgiveness and the Consuming Flame of the Ascended Masters, freeing me forever from all but the Perfection of the "I AM."

"I AM"! the Ascended Masters' Eternal, Complete and Unconditional Forgiveness and Forgetfulness of all human creation, past, present and future, and the replacement of it by the Full Perfection of the Ascended Masters forever.

"I AM" always proof against any sudden disturbance!

✧

"I AM"! Inexhaustible Energy!
"I AM"! Irresistible Divine Love!
"I AM"! Indestructible Health!
"I AM"! Inescapable Prosperity!
"I AM"! Invincible Protection!

"I AM"! the "Mighty Presence" on guard every second this day, instantly annihilating all that seeks to disturb, and holding my full God Dominion in this place forever.

"I AM" superior to discord; I can't afford to be bothered.

"I AM"! the Commanding Presence!
"I AM"! the Conquering Presence!
"I AM"! the Victorious Presence!
"I AM"! the Majestic Presence!
"I AM"! the Ascended Presence!

✧ ✧ ✧

"I AM"! the Presence of enough Love to release and reveal the Almightiness of the Great God-Self, "I AM"! forever.

"I AM"! the one Eternal, Self-sustained Life in action, ever expanding Perfection.

"I AM" the "Presence" producing abundance wherever I choose to use it, in the Service of Perfection—the Light.

In the Name of the "Mighty I AM Presence," the Ascended Masters and the "Light of God That Never Fails," all discordant activity within America shall cease, now and forever!

The "Presence" that "I AM" clothes these, my Beloved Ones, in their Eternal Transcendent Garments of Light.

The "Presence" that "I AM" clothes me now in my Eternal Transcendent Garment of Light.

O Blessed Flame of Divine Love, "I AM" Thy Pure Presence forever.

"I AM"! the All-Knowing, Dazzling, Fathomless Mind of God, the "Mighty I AM Presence"! Its

Almighty Intelligence, Its Boundless Knowledge, Its Limitless Wisdom, Its Infinite Inspiration, Its Eternal Truth, Its Full Illumination, Its Complete Perfection and Invincible Protection, releasing through me now Transcendent Ideas of Perfection from the Secret Heart of God, that have never come forth before anywhere in the Universe.

"I AM"! the Presence of Divine Love blessing everybody and everything in this business into Perfection, instantly and eternally manifest with Full Power.

"I AM"! every deal closed that brings Perfection to those buying these _____.

"I AM"! the Ascended Master Ease, Peace, Comfort, Purity, Control, and Conservation of all the Energy in my being and world forever.

Every day, speak to your body! Command it to be strong, receptive only to the Ascended Master Consciousness, to be a Perfect Expression of the Divine Presence of the "Mighty I AM," and to take on Its Beauty of form and expression:

"I AM" the "Light of God That Never Fails" now made permanently manifest in my flesh, as self-luminosity in Blazing Glory.

The "Mighty I AM Presence" is the only Healing Presence; and through It, I have the right to command all outer activity to be silent and obey my command.

⟡ ◇ ⟡

"Choose ye this day whom ye shall serve."

⟡ ◇ ⟡

To dismiss discord say:

    'Tis a wave on the ocean of human emotion,
    It's nothing, it's nothing at all;
    It comes like a flicker
    And goes away quicker
    When I on my God-Self do call.
    It is only a cloud
    But I say aloud,
    "I AM" the Sun! Don't you see?
    I blaze the Light!
    You fade from sight!
    And all things now obey me.
    (*Or:* The Light yields all things to me.)

People are bound because
they bind others.

✧ ✧ ✧

SALUTATIONS

THE LOVE STAR–*"The All"*

The Love Star, the Flame Breath,
　　The Great Heart in all,
Comes forth in Its Splendor
　　To answer each Call;
Reveals now Its Vict'ry,
　　In all Realms Its Light,
Clothes us in Its Glory
　　And Radiance bright;
Let all then surrender
　　Their might and their power,
Through loving Obedience
　　Be raised now this hour.
Forevermore Master!
　　Eternally free!
The Blest "I AM Presence,"
　　The Great Cosmic Key.

THE GREAT COSMIC BEING, SURYA

Surya, Surya, Surya!
Thou Great Blessed God from the Sun!
Surya, Surya, Surya!
Blaze forth Thy Great Light–make all One!
Surya, Surya, Surya!
Make us like Thyself–all Divine!
Surya, Surya, Surya!
Come through! We are evermore Thine.

THE LORD, THE MAHA CHOHAN

Maha Chohan! Maha Chohan! Maha Chohan! raise us all into Thy dazzling Jesus Christ Illumination, that we may become that Blazing White Light that draws all mankind upward until they become that Great Light also.

THE SILENT WATCHER
(Sung to the melody of *Absent* by Metcalf)

O Silent Watcher
    of Infinity!
Great Brooding Presence,
    All dwell within Thee;
Boundless Thy Love
    In earth, and sky, and sea;
O Silent Watcher,
    Thy Great God Self we see.

O Silent Watcher,
    Great God from the Sun!
I feel Thy Love,
    For Thou and I are One.
Shed forth Thy Light,
    Let all Thy Love now be;
O Silent Watcher,
    Through all Eternity.

O Silent Watcher,
    Blessed Self of me!
O Love Divine,
    Thy Light in all I see;
Thou Great God Presence,
    Evermore just Thee;
O Silent Watcher,
    O Love, now speak to me.

O Silent Watcher,
    Lord of Love Supreme!
From Thy Great Heart
    In one Unending Stream,
Thy Great Light flows
    From Thee, Great Sun above;
O Silent Watcher,
    Thou art the Self of Love.

✧ ✧ ✧

THE ARCHANGEL MICHAEL,
LORD OF THE SUN

Thou Archangel Michael,
    Lord of the Sun,
I hold my hand high to Thee,
    Thou Holy Great One!
I love Thee, I bless Thee,
    Thou God of Great Might!
Blaze through me, blaze through me,
    Blaze through me Thy Light!
Illumine, perfect me,
    Raise me to Thy Height;
Thou Archangel Michael,
    The Lord of the Sun!

THE
"I AM PRESENCE"
SPEAKS

I come on the Wings of the Great God Flame
    Into the seeming night.
I wend My Way through infinite space
    Raised high on My Pinions bright.
I bless, I heal, I illumine all things
    With the Radiance of God's own Might.
I blaze, I shine, I call "I AM"!
    The "Diamond Heart of Light!"

I breathe the Perfume of Life Supreme,
    The Glory of God's Delight;
I build, I mold, I guide Life's Stream,
    All beauty I bring to sight.
I dance, I play, I give to all
    Great Jewels from the far, far Height;
I come, I go, I answer each Call
    That looks in Love toward the Light.

✧

THE "PRESENCE"

"I AM" the "Presence,"
  the Great Eternal One,
"I AM" the "Presence,"
  from the Great, Great Central Sun;
"I AM" the "Presence,"
  the Secret Heart of Light,
"I AM" the "Presence,"
  the Love Flame blazing bright.

LIGHT

"I AM" *all* Light! *All* Light am I,
 In earth and air and sea and sky;
"I AM" the Light of Christ held high!
"I AM" *all* Light! *All* Light am I.

✧ ✧ ✧

ACKNOWLEDGMENT

Beloved Great God Self,
    Come, blaze Thou through me,
Reveal now Thy Presence,
    Thy Full Mastery.

Pour through me Thy Love Flame,
    My Light Self Supreme!
In Vict'ry transcendent,
    Thou "Mighty I AM."

ONENESS

O my Divinity,
Blend Thou with me
That I may blaze forth
Thy Full Victory.
Pour through me Thy Flame,
Thou God Self Supreme,
In Glory Transcendent,
Thou "Mighty I AM."

———— ◇ ◇ ◇ ————

ACCEPTANCE

"I AM" the deepest Love of God
In Thee, O Holy Blessed One;
"I AM" the Love within Thy Ray,
Thou Golden, Blazing Central Sun!

I feel Thy Breath, Thy Love, Thy Power,
Thy Light enfolds me every hour;
I lift my wings, my Victory won,
And rise now free! Life's journey done.

I fly with Thee throughout all space,
I gaze upon Thee face to face;
I know Thy Love is all of me,
Thou art myself, and "I AM" Thee.

———— ◇ ◇ ◇ ————

PROTECTION

O Blest "I AM," my way is clear,
    Thy Love Supreme stands ever near;
Thy Glorious Presence, "Great I AM,"
    Forever is my own God Flame.
Steadfast I stand now facing Thee
    And naught can interfere with me;
Thy blazing Love does now enfold
    And I Thy very Hand do hold.

The Love that "I AM" greets the Love in you,
And all Love, Light and Perfection come
Instantly through and bless you forever.

THE WAY

"I AM" the "Presence," the Great Eternal One,
"I AM" the Power, the Blazing Central Sun;
"I AM" the Splendor, the Dazzling Rays of Light,
"I AM" the Victory, through Love's All-glorious
    Might.

RELEASE

I come with Love in the Heart of me,
My Love flows out like a great calm sea;
My Love protects, setting all now free,
For Love "I AM," and "I AM" is Thee.

BLESSING FOR FOOD

"Mighty I AM Presence," accept this food, make it pure and holy. Transmute it into Thy Violet Golden Flame of Divine Love, and see that It purifies and perfects all our bodies with the speed of thought, forever Self-sustained.

MIRACLES

"I AM" these Mighty Miracles
    performed through me today!
"I AM" these Mighty Miracles
    from within my own God Ray!
"I AM" these Mighty Miracles
    come forth in Love to stay!
"I AM" these Mighty Miracles,
    the Ascended Masters' Way.

✧

PEACE

I rest serene in Thy Embrace,
I hold Thy Hand, I see Thy Face;
I know each day is under grace,
"I AM" at One with Thee.

"MIGHTY I AM PRESENCE"

Charge, charge, charge,
The Lightning of Thy Love;
Charge, charge, charge!
Raise all in Light above;
Charge, charge, charge!
Let all Thy Presence prove;
Charge, charge, charge!
Thy Love where e'er I move.

Take your full Authority, as a Child of Light! a Son of God! a Being of Living Fire, and rebuke every human creation by the command:

Peace! Peace! Peace! Be still!
"I AM" all Love!
"I AM" all Light!
All doeth now My Will.

(MELODY: "My Bonnie Lies Over the Ocean")

I love Thee, I love Thee, I love Thee!
I love Thee, My Dear Self—that's true;
My Holy, Great Glorious, Real Self,
This old human veil I've stepped through.

Chorus

Thyself—myself
I come now! I come now to You! to You;
Myself—Thyself
Blaze through me! blaze through me,
    blaze through.

I love You, I love You, I love You!
My Real Self, My God Self, I do;
My Holy Great Glorious, Light Self,
Blaze through me! blaze through me,
    blaze through.

Chorus

Thyself—myself,
I love You, I love You, I do, I do;
Myself! Thyself,
There's now only One! that One—You!

THE ASCENDED HOSTS' DECREE
FOR
AMERICA

In the Name and by the Power of the Ascended Hosts and the Ascended Master Saint Germain, I voice Their Decree for the Blessing and Protection of our Beloved America. America has been brought into being by the Ascended Hosts, as a Radiating Center to all the world for "the Light of God That Never Fails," in the age which has now begun.

Unto this end, there has been brought into existence a Sacred Document, upon which the Government of the United States of America has been founded. This is the Sacred Constitution of the United States of America. Therefore, it is the Decree of the Ascended Host that every official in our Government shall uphold and defend the Constitution of the United States of America unto the best of his ability, "So help him God."

Thus America shall go forward unto greater Glory than has ever been known on Earth. The Ascended Host, who are All-Powerful throughout the Universe, have decreed, "America shall remain at peace with the world." To those who have sought to draw America into the destruction unto which the rest of the nations of the Earth seem determined to open themselves, the Ascended Hosts have issued the All-Powerful Command that "America and Her people, those Beloved Children of God who have sought the Light, shall be protected; and that glory which they have earned shall go forth into manifestation."

Thus speaketh the Ascended Hosts unto the children of Earth! Their Decree goes forth unchallenged into manifestation from now on, henceforth and forevermore. In Their Name I have spoken!

Donald Ballard

FINIS

SERIES